Personal Notes:

Preface

WELCOME WORDS FROM JF BROU

Dear Self-Explorer,

I hope you are ready because I'm bringing you along for a ride filled with deep emotional flips, spiritual sharp turns, and a self-growth journey of ups and downs leading you to so many eye-opening contents and concepts toward your best version.

I'm proud of you! By taking this book, you have gone a long way already.

I love you so much. You are part of my family now.

The total workbook takes 6 to 8 hours to complete. I advise blocking 4 periods of 1.5-2 hours to finish it on a time frame of 7-10 days, other wise this will fall at the bottom of your to-do list. I also advise re-reading your answers quickly once a week to keep all of this strongly in your consciousness and attract positive results. Lastly, it is relevant to completely redo this workbook every 2-3 years.

Let's go. Take action and finish the workbook in depth.

Your new life has just begun.

"YOU DON'T KNOW WHAT YOU NEED IN YOUR LIFE UNTIL YOU FIGURE OUT WHO YOU ARE."

THE STORY BEHIND WHY I CREATED THIS WORKBOOK.

After launching my first business at 24 years old straight out of college, I've passed 5-6 years trying to find ways to grow without real success. From new marketing tactics to creating a kick-ass company culture, I always came back to the same pit hole. Until I realized I was the problem when some key insights came my way: "A business net worth will never outgrow the self-worth of its owners".

From that point, I started my psychological journey by hiring life coaches, taking personality tests, introspection exercises, and reading all the books that could help me fix myself to fix my situation.

With all the results, I asked myself how I became this way or another. That question led me to analyze my childhood, the famous crucial first 7 years. From many discoveries, I was able to analyze the trapped emotions affecting my energetic body, and this opened the doors to the spiritual world.

Through those last 9 years, I've learned so much about myself, the business world and the non-physical world. Today I'm confident I have a lot to give back to any young, driven individual reaching for the next level. If you need mentorship for your big dreams, I'll be super excited to help.

WHAT DOES IT MEAN TO BECOME YOUR BEST VERSION?

Everyone has a potential for greatness but there are so many barriers, obstacles, and environment conditioning between us and our higher self, so much that 97% of the population don't reach their potential. We get stuck in a matrix that wants us to follow the rules and consume to keep the economy circling.

Unfortunately, becoming your best version doesn't start with you but with how hard your parents worked to establish in you the right habits, and how supportive they were of your talents and interests. And finally, how conscious they were of their own demons and conditioning. But we can't change the past, so let's make the most of what we have been raised with. Everyone has a shot at their higher self no matter how late you start the work. It might take you longer but you'll end up stronger from your persistence of never giving up.

THE PHILOSOPHY BEHIND THE SYSTEM OF THE WORKBOOK.

Yes, you could just go right away and write a 3-year vision for your life. On top of it, most of us already have a vision of our future in our head, so it's easy and it will help improve it as we get more ideas while writing it. But what if you have a vision that is not entirely coming from you, some pieces might have been sold to you by the society, the media, advertisers, or even your parents. What if you take on a vision for selfish reasons, subconsciously seeking love and attention of others because of a small childhood traumatic episode that blocked some emotions and thickened your heart chakra wall.

That's why we need to go step by step and not jump straight to the final goal. We need to go deep and ask ourselves uncomfortable questions to go back to who we truly are before we got programmed by our environment.

Here are the steps:
First, personality tests will help you understand your tools and capabilities with what you are playing within this game of life.

Secondly, introspection exercise will help you understand your subconscious patterns, beliefs, fears, etc., everything blocking your progress to the next level.

Thirdly, we'll make an investigation of your life situation right now by analyzing your 7 wheels of life dimensions.

Fourth, we'll pick only one life dimension that we'll tackle on improving throughout the next 90 days. The only way to grow is to build the right habits.

Fifth, we'll bring clarity to your reason to wake up, bringing you full excitement each day.

Sixth, with all that baggage collected you'll be able to build a strong and magical vision for your life.

Seventh, we need to analyze what would happen if you don't take consistent actions on your vision, you'll most likely stay at the same place or worse. This will be your hell vision.

Finally, having a vision for your life is not all that you need, you won't be happier when you achieve that vision. Happiness is found in every moment of peace in being grateful for what you have, so we'll reinforce yours now with affirmations, gratitude enumeration, and a self-love letter.

Now you have all the tools to become your best version.

Personal Notes:

Rookie Mode
PERSONALITY TESTS

LEVEL 1 :

🕐 1 hour,
30 minutes
to complete

Today, personality tests have become a $400 million-a-year industry and are used in a range of contexts, including individual and relationship counseling, career planning, employee selection, and development, etc.

1.1. 16 PERSONALITIES (MBTI) NOTE

🕐 15 minutes to complete | https://www.16personalities.com/

The most common personality test used worldwide. It helps you learn about your strengths & weaknesses, romantic relationships, friendships, parenthood, career path, workplace habits, and more.

The MBTI measures your personality across four preferences. It will measure whether you interact with the outside world as an introvert or an extrovert, whether you process information with a sensing preference or an intuitive preference, whether you prefer to make decisions by thinking or feeling, or whether you go about things using a judging preference or a perceiving preference.

The most important thing is to be highly aware of your weaknesses so they don't put you in communication problems with your coworkers, friends, family, or spouse.

My personality: ....

Introvert/Extrovert level: ....

Observant/Intuitive level: ....

Thinking/Feeling level: ....

Judging/Prospecting level: ....

Assertive/Turbulent level: ....

WHAT'S YOUR PERSONALITY TYPE?

Use the questions on the outside of the chart ot determine the four letters of your Myers-Briggs type.
For each pair of letters, choose the side that seems most natural to you,
even if you don't agree with every description.

1. ARE YOU OUTWARDLY OR INWARDLY FOCUSED? IF YOU:

• Could be described as talkative, outgoing • Like to be in a fast-paced environment • Tend to work out ideas with others, think out loud • Enjoy being the center of attention	• Could be described as reserved, private • Prefer a slower pace with the time for contemplation • Tend to think things through inside your head • Would rather observe than be the center of attention
then you prefer	then you prefer
E EXTRAVERSION	**I** INTROVERSION

2. HOW DO YOU PREFER TO TAKE IN INFORMATION? IF YOU:

• Focus on the reality of how things are • Pay attention to concrete facts and details • Prefer ideas that have practical applications • Like to describe things in a specific, literal way	• Imagine the possibilities of how things could be • Notice the big picture, see how everything connects • Enjoy ideas and concepts for their own sake • Like to describe things in a figurative, poetic way
then you prefer	then you prefer
S SENSING	**N** INTUITION

3. HOW DO YOU PREFER TO MAKE DECISIONS? IF YOU:

• Make decisions in an impersonal way, using logical reasoning • Value justice, fairness • Enjoy finding the flaws in an argument • Could be described as reasonable, level-headed	• Base your decisions on personal values and how your actions affect others • Value harmony, forgiveness • Like to please others point out the best in people • Could be described as warm, empathetic
then you prefer	then you prefer
T THINKING	**F** FEELING

4. HOW DO YOU PREFER TO LIVE YOUR OUTER LIFE? IF YOU:

• Prefer to have matters settled • Think rules and deadlines should be respected • Prefer to have detailed, step-by-step instructions • Make plans, want to know what you're getting into	• Prefer to leave your options open • See rules and deadlines as flexible • Like to improvise and make things up as you go • Are spontaneous, enjoy surprises and new situations
then you prefer	then you prefer
J JUDGING	**P** PERCEIVING

ISTJ
Responsible, sincere, analytical, reserved, realistic, systematic. Hardworking and trustworthy with sound practical judgment.

ISFJ
Warm, considerate, gentle, responsible, pragmatic, thorough. Devoted caretakers who enjoy being helpful to others.

INFJ
Idealistic, organized, insightful, dependable, compassionate, gentle. Seek harmony and cooperation, enjoy intellectual stimulation.

INTJ
Innovative, independent, strategic, logical, reserved, insightful. Driven by their own original ideas to achieve improvements.

ISTP
Action-oriented, logical, analytical, spontaneous, reserved, independent. Enjoy adventure, skilled at understanding how mechanical things work.

ISFP
Gentle, sensitive, nurturing, helpful, flexible, realistic. Seek to create a personal environment that is both beautiful and practical.

INFP
Sensitive creative, idealistic, perceptive, caring, loyal. Value inner harmony and personal growth, focus on dreams and possibilities.

INTP
Intellectual, logical, precise, reserved, flexible, imaginative. Original thinkers who enjoy speculation and creative problem solving.

ESTP
Outgoing, realistic, action-oriented, curious, versatile, spontaneous. Pragmatic problem solvers and skillful negotiators.

ESFP
Playful, enthusiastic, friendly, spontaneous, tactful, flexible. Have strong common sense, enjoy helping people in tangible ways.

ENFP
Enthusiastic, creative, spontaneous, optimistic, supportive, playful. Value inspiration, enjoy starting new projects, see potential in others.

ENTP
Inventive, enthusiastic, strategic, enterprising, inquisitive, versatile. Enjoy new ideas and challenge, value inspiration.

ESTJ
Efficient, outgoing, analytical, systematic, dependable, realistic. Like to run the show and get things done in an orderly fashion.

ESFJ
Friendly, outgoing, reliable, conscientious, organized, practical. Seek to be helpful and please others, enjoy being active and productive.

ENFJ
Caring, enthusiastic, idealistic, organized, diplomatic, responsible. Skilled communicators who value connection with people.

ENTJ
Strategic, logical, efficient, outgoing, ambitious, independent. Effective organizers of people and long-range planners.

2 best relationships match (In blue on the relationship chart):

....

....

SIMPLIFIED MYERS BRIGGS TYPE COMPATIBILITY CHART

Columns (left to right): INFP, ENFP, INFJ, ENFJ, INTJ, ENTJ, INTP, ENTP, ISFP, ESFP, ISTP, ESTP, ISFJ, ESFJ, ISTJ, ESTJ

Rows (top to bottom): INFP, ENFP, INFJ, ENFJ, INTJ, ENTJ, INTP, ENTP, ISFP, ESFP, ISTP, ESTP, ISFJ, ESFJ, ISTJ, ESTJ

CHART LEGEND

- Uh-Oh, Think This One Through
- It Could Work, But Not Ideal
- One Sided Match
- It's Got a Good Chance
- Often Listed as an Ideal Match

Actors/famous person with your first best match personality type (Google it):

_____

_____

_____

Actors/famous person with your second best match personality type (Google it):

....

....

....

MY STRENGTHS:	MY WEAKNESSES:
1	1 ....
2	2 ....
3	3 ....
4	4 ....
5	5 ....
6	6 ....

CAREER PATH:

Describe your ideal workplace environment:

....

....

List career roles suitable for your personality:

....

....

Describe your ideal situation with systems, hierarchy, and management style:

....

....

WORKPLACE HABITS:

Describe your ideal situation with subordinates, colleagues, and managers:

....

....

....

....

1.2. HEXACO

🕐 15 minutes to complete | http://hexaco.org/

People with higher than average agreeableness and low conscientiousness make amazing coworkers and build a supportive company culture, but they need to be pushed all the time to reach their goals.

People with higher than average conscientiousness and low agreeableness make high achievers, they want to reach goals and push the company forward but might be teammates' problems in the long run to build the right company culture.

If you have highly agreeable and conscientious employees/coworkers, make sure you treat them well to keep them long term, they are your best team members.

	RESULT	MEDIAN
AGREEABLENESS		3.00
Forgivingness		2.75
Gentleness		3.25
Flexibility		2.75
Patience		3.25

	RESULT	MEDIAN
CONSCIENTIOUSNESS		3.47
Organization		3.38
Diligence		3.88
Perfectionism		3.63
Prudence		3.25

Top 3 sub-traits that are your strengths.

1 .... Result: ....

2 .... Result: ....

3 .... Result: ....

Top 3 sub-traits you should be working on.

1 .... Result: ....

2 .... Result: ....

3 .... Result: ....

1.3. DARK TRIAD

🕐 5 minutes to complete | https://openpsychometrics.org/tests/SD3/

Known as the antisocial test, every entrepreneur, actor, model, or stripper starts their journey with very high Machiavellianism and high narcissism.

Percentile goes from 0-84 with 12 as a low score, 30 as average, and everything above 45 should be taken in attention to be solved. High scores on those traits come from childhood trauma or just something you perceived wrongly, most likely at the age of 3 to 4. The subconscious mind builds itself in the first 5 years of our lives. Doing an Ayahuasca retreat can help you remember those childhood events.

People with a high percentile on these traits seek short-term relationships, they are more into one-night stands and friends with benefits.

TRAIT	RESULT	PERCENTILE
NARCISSISM (Confidence/Ego factor) Talk about themself, creative, intelligent		
MACHIAVELLIANISM (Cunning/Sneakiness factor) Bullied as a child, manipulative, opportunist, hide their true motive, exploit people, white-collar crime		
PSYCHOPATHY (Courage/Ruthlessness factor) No emotions, lack of empathy, blue-collar crime		

1.4. DISC

🕐 15 minutes to complete | https://www.123test.com/disc-personality-test/

This measures your personality on a **Dominant/Driver** scale, **Inspiring/Influencing** scale, **Steadiness/Supportive** scale, and **Collective/Consciousness** scale. Each scale measures different characteristics, each has its own strengths and weaknesses. Typically speaking, you will score higher on one or two of the traits, making that your personality type.

DOMINANT/DRIVER
Project Managers, Operation, Directors, Consultants
Driven, dominate a conversation, directing audience, good at giving direction, good at getting stuff done, good with deadlines, make things happen.
READY, FIRE, AIM
Focusing on getting things done.

INSPIRING/INFLUENCING
Media, News, TV, Speakers, Visionary
Influencer comes up with new ideas and insights, great at inspiring people to make changes, persuasion, negotiation, have an impact.
READY, TALK, TALK
Focused on making sure people like what is being done.

STEADINESS/SUPPORTIVE
Psychiatrist, Psychologist
Stable, mediator, great at making sure everyone is connected, getting good at making teams work effectively together, good at lining out issues and touchy points in areas of challenges. People in the organization you go get a hug from. People that give a lot of love.
TALK, TALK, TALK
Focused on making the team work well together.

COLLECTIVE/CONSCIOUSNESS
Analytics, Producers, Testers, Coders
Calm, conscious, cautious, detail-oriented, quality, perfectionist
AIM, AIM, AIM
Focused on making sure the quality has been done well.

* You need ALL 4 D I S C to make an effective team.
** Can be 2 at the same time but better focus on improving your best one.
*** They are all good leaders, just different types of leaders.

Your Results:

_____

_____

_____

_____

1.5. YOUR 5 LOVE LANGUAGES

🕐 10 minutes to complete | http://www.5lovelanguages.com/

Most important

1 _____ Result: _____

2 _____ Result: _____

3 _____ Result: _____

4 _____ Result: _____

5 _____ Result: _____

1. **WORDS OF AFFIRMATION:** Typically, words of appreciation or praise—thanking someone for the different ways that they show love or praising someone for who they are, what they do, and what you appreciate about them.
2. **ACTS OF SERVICE:** Simple acts that help to make the other person's life easier or make things run smoother.
3. **RECEIVING GIFTS:** Almost always perceived as an act of love, but Chapman points out that people often don't realize that, for some, receiving gifts is the primary way through which they feel loved.
4. **QUALITY TIME:** Giving someone your undivided attention—putting away your phone and distractions and truly being with that person, whether that is having a conversation or going out and doing something together.
5. **PHYSICAL TOUCH:** Comes in many forms—holding hands, massaging, snuggling, etc. For some, physical touch is a very important expression of love. Of course, physical touch should always be communicated clearly and consensually!

1.6. NUMEROLOGY

Explore your numerology chart here: https://video.numerologist.com/

Life Path Number: ....
Describe your numerology personality:

....

....

....

Expression Number: ....

Soul Urge Number: ....

HERE ARE OTHER PERSONALITY TESTS I SUGGEST YOU DO IN YOUR SPARE TIME:

Enneagram
https://www.eclecticenergies.com/enneagram/test

Give and Take the quiz
http://www.adamgrant.net/selfgivertaker

Which flow profile are you
http://www.flowgenomeproject.com/free-flow-profile/

The Cube
http://www.getinhermind.com/sure-fire-routines/five-minute-personality-test-the-cube

Apprentice Mode
INTROSPECTION EXERCISES

WHEN ASKED,
"WHAT'S THE BIGGEST MISTAKE WE MAKE IN LIFE?"
THE BUDDHA REPLIED,
"THE BIGGEST MISTAKE IS THAT
YOU THINK YOU HAVE TIME."

2.1. QUALITIES OF PEOPLE YOU ADMIRE AND WEAKNESSES OF PEOPLE YOU DISLIKE

🕐 7 minutes to complete

List all the qualities of people you admire:

....

....

....

....

....

....

List all the weaknesses of people you dislike:

....

....

....

....

....

Over a 2-3-year period of analyzing and reading this, you might tend to end up more on one side than the other.

2.2. IDEAL NEIGHBORHOOD

🕐 5 minutes to complete

Write down all the people from all walks of life, dead or alive, that you would like to invite at any time to enjoy a conversation around coffee or tea and write down why. What is the criteria of that person you would enjoy to have at your convenience for advice or reconfort.

....

....

....

....

....

....

....

What are you realizing from this exercise?

....

....

....

....

11

2.3. CRITERIA OF YOUR IDEAL LIFE PARTNER

🕐 5 minutes to complete

List down all criteria of your dream life partner, it will help you see what you need to work on. (Based on the 7 wellness life dimensions: Physical, Personal, Job, Business, Finance, Spiritual, Relationship.)

....

....

....

....

....

2.4. LIVES AUDIT

🕐 5 minutes to complete

Analyze everyone you had a physical or virtual conversation within the last month. List their name and grade them on 1 to 10 without using the number 7.

Evaluate them on how you felt after the conversation: energetic, happy, enthusiastic, or drained, stressed, demotivated, etc.

NAME	RESULT	NAME	RESULT	NAME	RESULT

2.5. GOOD HABITS & BAD HABITS

🕐 10 minutes to complete

List all your bad habits that are making you lose time, energy, money, relationships. We are creatures of habit, when you start micro analysing it you'll realize habits everywhere.

....

....

....

....

....

List all your GOOD habits you are proud of that give you an edge over other people:

....

....

....

....

....

....

....

....

2.6. LIST YOUR PARENTS' STRENGTHS AND WEAKNESSES

🕐 5 minutes to complete

The ones you hate the most, you most likely have them at a different level without being aware of it.

MOM'S STRENGTHS:		MOM'S WEAKNESSES:
1	1	
2	2	
3	3	

DAD'S STRENGTHS:		DAD'S WEAKNESSES:
1	1	
2	2	
3	3	

Your family MBTI (16 personalities)

MOM:

DAD:

BRO/SIS:

BRO/SIS:

2.7. BEST PROFESSIONAL SKILL

🕐 15 minutes to complete

Ask 10-20 of your current and past colleagues, "Hey, I'm doing an introspection exercise. What do you think is my strongest professional skill?"

You should improve that skill to become an expert at it. When you work 1 hour with that skill you provide the most return to your business or organization.

Summary:

Top 3 skills coming back from all the people you contacted:

1 ....

2 ....

3 ....

2.8. VALUES & VIRTUES

🕐 10 minutes to complete

List your top 10 values you live or would like to live by and then circle your top 3:

....

....

....

....

....

....

....

....

....

....

List your virtues to your top 3 values:
Behaviors that make you act on those values daily/weekly even if you are exhausted or have no time that day/week.

1 ....

2 ....

3 ....

2.9. ACTIVITIES YOU DON'T LIKE DOING (PERSONAL & PROFESSIONAL LIFE)

🕐 5 minutes to complete

....

....

....

....

2.10. WHAT TYPE OF TRIP/TRAVEL/EXPLORATION DO YOU LIKE?

🕐 5 minutes to complete

(Beach, adventure, nature, ancient civilization, history, architecture, art, landscape, sports, food, people, etc.)

....

....

....

....

List your 3 dream locations to take a trip to and explore and why.

....

....

....

2.11. TOP 5 MOVIES OF ALL TIME AND WHY?

🕐 5 minutes to complete

1 ....
2 ....
3 ....
4 ....
5 ....

2.12. LIST THE EMOTIONS YOU LIVED IN THE PAST WEEK? WHAT HAPPENED AND WHY?

🕐 5 minutes to complete

....

....

....

....

....

....

2.13. WHAT ARE YOUR CRAVINGS AND AVERSIONS?

🕐 5 minutes to complete

Cravings, powerful desire for something. What do you want now, what are you chasing?

....

....

....

....

....

Aversion, someone or something that arouses a strong dislike or disinclination:

2.14. WHAT ARE THE BEHAVIORS THAT ARE ROOTED IN YOUR EGO?

🕐 5 minutes to complete

Coming from the bestseller Principles from Ray Dalio, our 2 biggest enemies are our ego and our blind spots. What are the things you have been doing to get attention, love, recognition, fame, money, success, etc?

2.15. WHAT ARE YOUR BLIND SPOTS?

🕐 5 minutes to complete

Coming from the bestseller Principles from Ray Dalio, our 2 biggest enemies are our ego and our blind spots. What are the things you don't know, don't see, don't understand, and need to know to move to the next stage? What are the things that others see from their own eyes, world view, personalities that you don't?

....

....

....

....

....

2.16. LIST YOUR RESOURCES

🕐 10 minutes to complete

(knowledge, contacts, skills, colleagues, assets, experiences, materials, etc.)

....

....

....

....

....

....

3 free events/experiences I could offer with my resources to inspire/help humans:

....

....

....

3 next resources I want to acquire (investment on myself):

....

....

....

2.17. EXPOSE YOURSELF TO MENTORS. WORK FOR FREE FOR THEM

🕐 5 minutes to complete

3 persons I would "pay" $10k+ to work for:

1 .... why: ....

2 .... why: ....

3 .... why: ....

Choose a date that you will reach them all via all the channels possible, praising them for their work and influence on you and asking them a quick-to-answer question to start building a relationship.

2.18. FIND ROLE MODELS THAT ARE 10 YEARS AHEAD OF YOU

🕐 5 minutes to complete

1 .... industry: ....

2 .... industry: ....

3 .... industry: ....

4 .... industry: ....

5 .... industry: ....

2.19. WHAT WOULD YOU DO IF YOU KNEW YOU HAD 1 DAY, 1 WEEK, OR 1 MONTH TO LIVE?

🕐 5 minutes to complete

(What person would you praise? What trip would you take? What secret would you tell? What book would you write? What knowledge would you share? What community would you create? What show would you put on?)

1 day:

....

....

....

1 week:

....

....

....

1 month:

....

....

....

WHY are you not doing those things right now?

....

....

2.20. FACING YOUR FEARS

🕐 30 minutes to complete

The premeditation of evils. List down your top fear at the moment that is stopping you from growing to your best self. Start the sentence with What if I... lose my parents, quit my job, leave my relationship, jump from a plane, do Ayahuasca, travel the world for 1 year, quit college, start a business, don't pay my debt, etc.

Watch "Why you should define your fears instead of your goals." | Tim Ferriss

Read "The ultimate guide to face ALL your hidden fears."
https://medium.com/@jfbrou/the-ultimate-guide-to-face-all-your-hidden-fears-4ef72ced1521

1. **DEFINE**
   What if I... (list your fears)

   ....

   ....

   Really ask yourself why you are feeling that way to arrive at the bottom core.

   Write 10 worst things that could happen.

   1 ....   6 ....
   2 ....   7 ....
   3 ....   8 ....
   4 ....   9 ....
   5 ....   10 ....

2. **PREVENT**
   How can you prevent these episodes or reduce the likelihood of them happening?

   ....

   ....

   ....

3. **REPAIR**
   What could I do to repair the damage if my fear happens? Has anyone else in the history of time figured this out? What would be the benefits of an attempt or partial success? What are the possible good outcomes if you take action?

   ....

   ....

   ....

   ....

   ....

   ....

4. COST OF INACTION

If I avoid these actions, what would my life would look like?
(Emotionally, physically, financially, etc.)

In 6 months

....

....

In 1 year

....

....

In 3 years

....

....

Thinker Mode
PAST, PRESENT, FUTURE

"LIFE IS 10% WHAT HAPPENS TO YOU
AND 90% HOW YOU REACT TO IT."

ANALYZE YOUR PAST
🕐 30 minutes to complete

3.1. WHAT ARE YOUR ACCOMPLISHMENTS FROM YOUR LAST WEEK?

🕐 10 minutes to complete

(Analyze in each of your 7 wellness life dimensions.) (How many times you help friends, talk to your family, how many tasks you get done, how long you learn about your industry, how long you workout, what you eat, when you meditate, what did you write in your self-development journal, etc.)

3.2. WHEN AND WHAT DID YOU START AND NEVER FINISHED?

🕐 5 minutes to complete

....

....

....

....

3.3. WHICH BIG DECISIONS HAVE YOU MADE OUT OF LOVE AND FEAR?

🕐 10 minutes to complete

LOVE:

....

....

....

....

FEAR:

....

....

....

....

3.4. LOVE BEGINS AT HOME. WHO IN THE FAMILY HAS BEEN UNWANTED, UNLOVED, UNCARED FOR, OR FORGOTTEN IN THE PAST?

Ask yourself why and put yourself in their shoes.

🕐 10 minutes to complete

....

....

....

....

3.5. WHAT ARE YOUR BIGGEST REGRETS?

🕐 5 minutes to complete

....

....

....

....

3.6. WHAT SHOULD YOU HAVE SAID NO TO IN THE PAST?

🕐 5 minutes to complete

....

....

....

....

3.7. WHAT'S YOUR GREATEST ACCOMPLISHMENT THAT YOU ARE THE PROUDEST OF?

🕐 5 minutes to complete

3.8. WHAT HAS BEEN YOUR MOST CHALLENGING SITUATION SO FAR?

🕐 5 minutes to complete

3.9. WHEN WAS THE LAST TIME YOU STRONGLY PUSHED YOURSELF OUT OF YOUR COMFORT ZONE?

🕐 5 minutes to complete

3.10. WHAT WAS THE BEST DAY OF YOUR LIFE AND WHY?

🕐 5 minutes to complete

....
....
....
....
....

3.11. WHAT DID YOU WANT TO BE WHEN YOU WERE 8-12 YEARS OLD?

🕐 5 minutes to complete

....
....
....
....
....

NOW
🕐 45 minutes to complete

3.12. WHAT WOULD YOU DO IF YOU WERE GIVEN 10 MILLION DOLLARS NOW?

🕐 5 minutes to complete

....
....
....
....
....

3.13. WHAT ARE THE BOOKS YOU'LL KEEP AND LEAVE BEHIND TO YOUR CHILDREN AND LITTLE CHILDREN?

🕐 5 minutes to complete

3.14. WHAT WOULD PEOPLE BE SURPRISED TO KNOW ABOUT YOU?

🕐 5 minutes to complete

3.15. WHEN YOU THINK OF SUCCESS, WHO IS THE FIRST PERSON THAT COMES TO MIND AND WHY?

🕐 5 minutes to complete

3.16. WHAT'S THE BEST ADVICE YOU EVER GOT?

🕐 5 minutes to complete

....

....

....

....

3.17. WHAT ARE YOUR DAILY WORRIES OR THINGS YOU ARE SCARED OF HAPPENING ON A DAILY BASIS?

🕐 5 minutes to complete

(Talking to a beautiful girl in the street, dancing in public, being late, not having enough money, talking to someone you don't connect with, not fully living, etc.)

....

....

....

....

3.18. WHAT DREAM COMES BACK OFTEN WHEN YOU SLEEP?

🕐 5 minutes to complete

(What are the symbols in it.)

....

....

....

....

3.19. AT 80 YEARS OLD ON YOUR DEATHBED, WHAT COULD BE YOUR LIFE REGRETS AND WHAT WOULD YOU TELL YOUR 20 SOMETHING SELF?

🕐 5 minutes to complete

....

....

....

....

....

3.20. LIST 20 THINGS YOU WOULD LIKE TO DO BEFORE YOU DIE

🕐 5 minutes to complete

1		11	
2		12	
3		13	
4		14	
5		15	
6		16	
7		17	
8		18	
9		19	
10		20	

3.21. WHAT ARE YOUR 3-YEAR, 5-YEAR, 10-YEAR, 20-YEAR, 30-YEAR DREAMS?

🕐 15 minutes to complete

3-year:

5-year:

10-year:

20-year:

30-year:

3.22. WHAT WILL BE YOUR LEGACY?

🕐 10 minutes to complete

(Impact on others, known for when you are gone)

Warrior Mode
EMOTIONS

Emotions are the subject that will free you from all your suffering. 93% of humans have a heart wall that developed from trapped emotions lived in the first 7 years of their lives. The heart wall is a metaphor meaning that your heart chakra opens and closes easily many times a day with your thoughts and reaction to life situations. Your heart chakra is the center core where all the energy of love come in and out. A blocked heart chakra will lead you to act out of fear.

Your trapped emotions are relived over and over again through your life each time a situation triggers them. The thing is we naturally think it's that specific situation that makes us react like that, but it's only a trigger to hit something that's been sleeping inside.

Trapped emotions create balls of energy in specific organs of your body that, over the years, start ripping tissues off these organs. From Chinese Traditional Medicine (TCM), we have 5 core organs trapping 5 types of emotions which is not letting the Qi energy (the vital energy, energy of love) circulate properly through those organs. New theories think that this is the cause of every cancer. Watch the documentary Heal on Netflix and E-motions on Gaia.

Dr. Bradley Nelson invented a legendary technique to find our trapped emotions and open the gates to relive them, so we can release them for good. Using the muscle testing technique with the emotion code chart below, you can access your subconscious to find 5-6 emotions trapped in a one-hour session. You then usually relive those emotions in the next 1 to 5 days. You then go back on doing sessions after sessions with a few weeks interval.

Watch these videos to get a better understanding of the process.
- Bradley Nelson Demonstrates Muscle Testing and Emotion Code
- Emotion Code - Process of Releasing Trapped Emotion

THE EMOTION CODE™ CHART

	COLUMN A	COLUMN B
Row 1 Heart or Small Intestine	Abandonment Betrayal Forlorn Lost Love Unreceived	Effort Unreceived Heartache Insecurity Overjoy Vulnerability
Row 2 Spleen or Stomach	Anxiety Despair Disgust Nervousness Worry	Failure Helplessness Hopelessness Lack of Control Low Self-Esteem
Row 3 Lung or Colon	Crying Discouragement Rejection Sadness Sorrow	Confusion Defensiveness Grief Self-Abuse Stubbornness
Row 4 Liver or Gall Bladder	Anger Bitterness Guilt Hatred Resentment	Depression Frustration Indecisiveness Panic Taken for Granted
Row 5 Kidneys or Bladder	Blaming Dread Fear Horror Peeved	Conflict Creative Insecurity Terror Unsupported Wishy Washy
Row 6 Glands & Sexual Organs	Humiliation Jealousy Longing Lust Overwhelm	Pride Shame Shock Unworthy Worthlessness

I have a trapped emotion of .... from the age of ....

related with .... (person)
because of .... (situation).

I have a trapped emotion of .... from the age of ....

related with .... (person)
because of .... (situation).

I have a trapped emotion of .... from the age of ....

related with .... (person)
because of .... (situation).

I have a trapped emotion of .... from the age of ....

related with .... (person)
because of .... (situation).

I have a trapped emotion of .... from the age of ....

related with .... (person)
because of .... (situation).

Conqueror Mode

BELIEFS

"BELIEFS HAVE THE POWER TO CREATE AND
THE POWER TO DESTROY. HUMAN BEINGS HAVE
THE AWESOME ABILITY TO TAKE ANY EXPERIENCE
OF THEIR LIVES AND CREATE A MEANING THAT
DISEMPOWERS THEM OR ONE THAT CAN LITERALLY
SAVE THEIR LIVES."

~ TONY ROBBINS

Using the muscle testing technique again, circle the self-limiting beliefs you have below.

1. I deserve love.
2. I'm not good enough.
3. I need the recognition of others.
4. I don't have time.
5. I am not beautiful.
6. I don't have the knowledge.
7. Achieving will make me happy.
8. I am rich.
9. I can make everything I visualize happen.
10. I need support to move forward.
11. I need resources to grow my business.
12. I'm too young to be successful.
13. I'm a troubled son/daughter.

14. I need to strive for perfection.
15. I'm a failure.
16. Now is not the right time.
17. I am not ready.
18. There is too much competition.
19. People do not want what I have.
20. I don't want to be publicly ridiculed.
21. I need to go deep to show I'm better than others.
22. I fear to be abundant.
23. I fear to lose everything.
24. There's nothing after death.
25. I'll never be wealthy. Rich people are dishonest.
26. I'll never have enough money to have a nice house.
27. If I'm rich, people will try to steal from me.
28. My friends will treat me differently if I have a lot of money.

What are the top 3 self limited beliefs that you need to work on right now?

....

....

....

For more insights in self-limiting beliefs, read this article: https://medium.com/change-your-mind/how-to-identify-your-limiting-beliefs-and-get-rid-of-them-once-and-for-all-dafa4c477a9e

Analytics Mode
7 WHEELS OF LIFE DIMENSIONS

Every 90 days, on a level of 1 to 10 without using the number 7, your 7 wellness life dimensions. When you are not balanced on those 7 wellness life dimensions, no matter how hard you work, you'll always end up stuck in a crazy 8 loop over and over again because your wheel won't roll smoothly.

LIFE DIMENSION	RESULT
PERSONAL (give back/help/social/community)	
JOB (daily work, skills, position, domain)	
BUSINESS (team/organization/clients/industry)	
RELATIONSHIP (family/core friends/spouse & kids)	
PHYSICAL (body/health/mental)	
FINANCE (cash flow/savings/debt/expenses)	
SPIRITUAL inner-self/love/mindfulness/gratitude)	

Choose 1 that you will work on intensively in the next 90 days: ....

Would it improve other dimensions at the same time? ....

WHY? ....

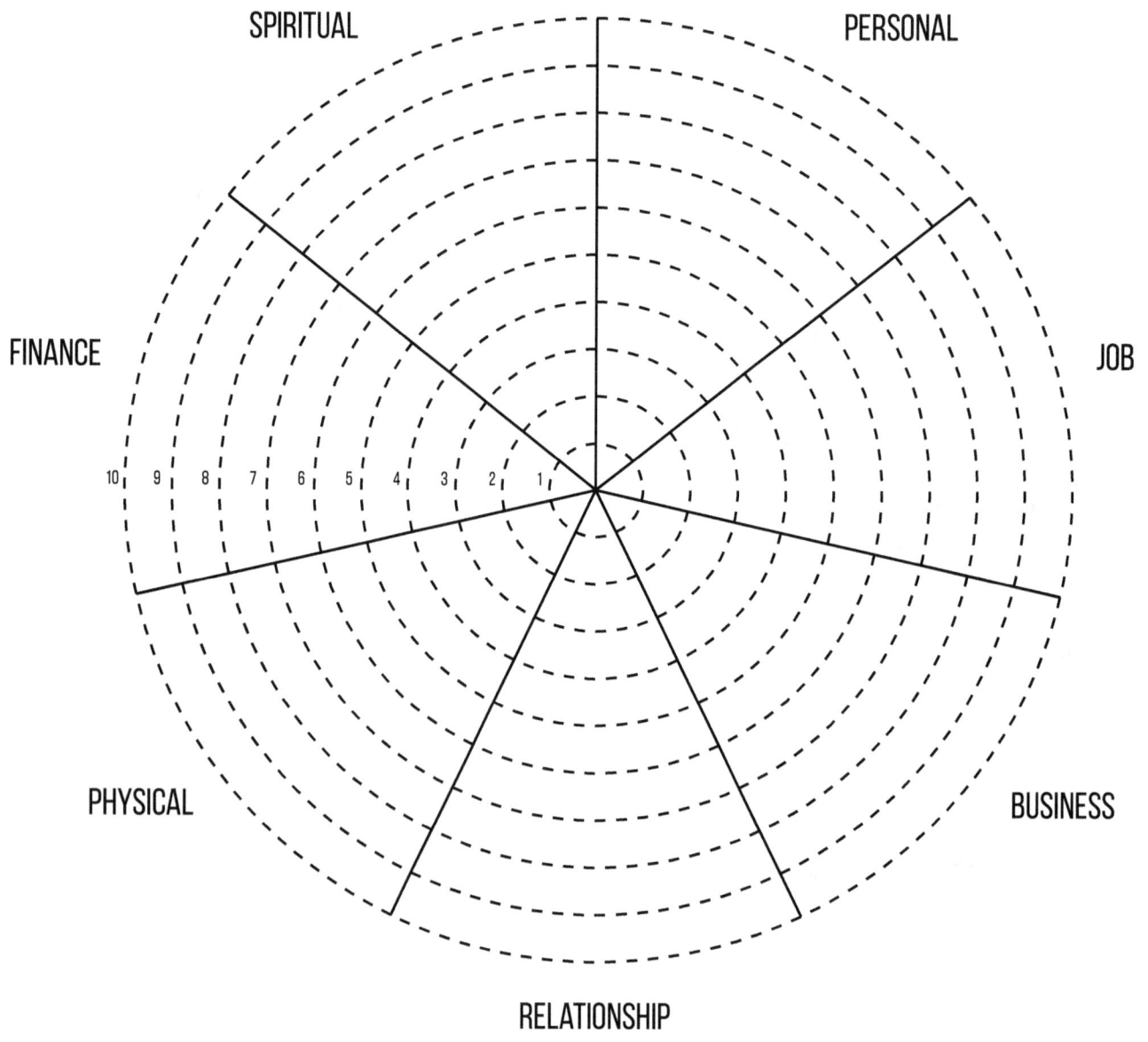

Planner Mode
90-DAY GOAL SETTING PLAN

Based on your 7 wellness life dimensions evaluation, choose one dimension you need to improve in the next 90 days that would improve two or three other dimensions at the same time. Ask yourself where you would like to be someday with this dimension.

GOAL SETTINGS TO THE NOW!

Someday Goal

What is the ONE THING I want to do someday?

....

....

Five-Year Goal

What is the ONE THING I need to do in five years to accomplish my someday goal?

....

....

One-Year Goal

What is the ONE THING I need to do in one year to accomplish my five-year goal?

....

....

One-Month Goal

What is the ONE THING I need to do in one month to accomplish my one-year goal?

....

....

One-Week Goal

What is the ONE THING I need to do in one week to accomplish my one-month goal?

....

....

Today Goal

What is the ONE THING I need to do today to accomplish my one-week goal?

....

....

Now Goal

What is the ONE THING I need to do now to accomplish my goal today?

....

Find the lead domino and whack away at it until it falls. The lead domino is the habit that will make many others fall. For example, running daily early in the morning will lead you to stop going out drinking, smoking, and eating fast food. The lead domino needs to be the smallest daily habit as stated by the Kaizen principle[1] that you will build for 66 days.

What is the minimum daily goal habit that will whack away other habits and improve this dimension you need to fix and might also improve 2 other wellness life dimensions?

I am committing on .... (specific habit)

for .... (minimum goal of kaizen principle).

My trigger to push me starting my habit is ....
(cue: LOCATION, TIME, EMOTIONS STATE, ACTIONS OF OTHER PEOPLE, IMMEDIATELY

PRECEDING LAST ACTIONS) and my reward after finishing is .... (reward)
that I slowly start craving this habit daily. I'm committing 66 days in a row to this habit to make it a lifestyle.

---

[1]   According to the Kaizen philosophy, a series of small improvements made continuously over a long period of time can result in drastic improvement in business processes. https://www.brighthubpm.com/project-planning/100172-explaining-the-kaizen-principle/

IKIGAI

A Japanese concept meaning 'a reason for being'

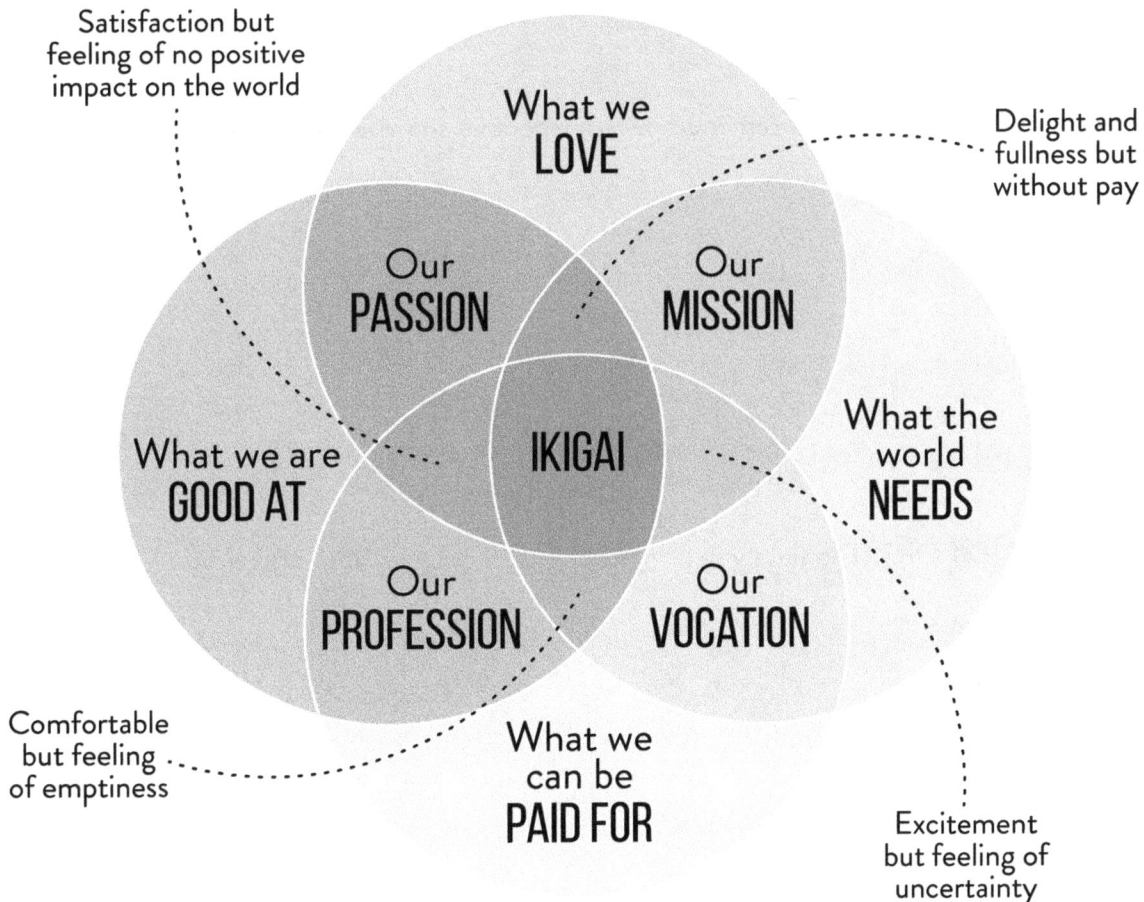

Satisfaction but feeling of no positive impact on the world

Delight and fullness but without pay

What we **LOVE**

Our **PASSION**

Our **MISSION**

What we are **GOOD AT**

IKIGAI

What the world **NEEDS**

Our **PROFESSION**

Our **VOCATION**

Comfortable but feeling of emptiness

What we can be **PAID FOR**

Excitement but feeling of uncertainty

8.1. IKIGAI = A REASON FOR BEING.

What do you LOVE? (In your personal and professional life, the contrary of what you hate.)

....

....

....

....

What are you GOOD AT? (What you're good at that you might like or not like to do.)

....

....

....

....

What does the WORLD NEED? (From your own perspective and vision of the world.)

....

....

....

....

What can I get PAID FOR? (The skills you bring to the table to grow your organization.)

....

....

....

....

8.2. QUADRANT OF SUCCESS.

What do you LOVE that you are good at? (PASSION)

....
....
....
....
....
....

What don't you LOVE that you are good at? (PAYING YOUR BILLS)

....
....
....
....
....
....

What do you LOVE but you are not good at yet? (POTENTIAL) (Learn more, not yet an expert.)

....
....
....
....
....
....

What don't you LOVE that you are not good at? (DAILY TASKS)

....
....
....
....
....
....

* We spend most of our lives on #3 and #4.
** #1 & #2 require deep investment and learning. You need to go all-in on those.

8.3. FIND YOUR WHY.

https://courses.startwithwhy.com/
The reasons you will NEVER give up. (Family, purpose, past suffering, life situation, etc.)

8.4. STATE YOUR PURPOSE IN ONE SENTENCE.

Reason to wake up and grow, serve people/the world, give back, inspire.

Discipline Mode
YOUR IDEAL SITUATIONS

9.1. MORNING ROUTINE

The objective of a morning routine is to create momentum to tackle your one thing of the day, the thing that will give you 80% of the results of the day on moving toward your 90-day goal.

Here's an example of a morning routine. I highly suggest starting with fewer things.

7:30:

"Wake up with Determination Alarm" motivation soundtrack

7:30—7:45:

1) Remove earplugs, fold the pillow in 2 to lift my head, get up to shut down the alarm, thoughts monitoring (10 min).
2) Go pee, smile in the mirror, happy vibe music, drink cold water, brush teeth reverse hand.
3) 1-minute workout, yoga stretching.

7:45—8:20:

4) Make my bed and 5 minutes journal affirmation, positive statement, love, gratitude and 1 goal setting.
5) 10 minutes of bodyweight or jump rope workout.

8:20—8:50:

6) Cold shower
7) Get dressed, do my hair, cream, perfume, etc. Get ready to go out.
8) Drink cold-pressed green juice and eat fruits.
9) Review 3-year vision, tasks, and goals of the day and week.

NOT TO DO LIST:

Don't have a big breakfast or coffee before your one thing.
Don't leave the house without spending 1 hour 30 minutes on your one thing.
Don't open communication apps or anything that can infiltrate your peace.

CREATE YOUR MORNING ROUTINE.

The goal is to have at least 2 things every 20 minutes for a morning routine of 1 hour.

7:30: "Wake up with Determination Alarm" motivation soundtrack

First 20 minutes: From .... to .... (time):

....

....

....

Second 20 minutes: From .... to .... (time):

....

....

....

Third 20 minutes: From .... to .... (time):

....

....

....

NOT TO DO LIST:

....

....

....

9.2. NIGHT ROUTINE

The objective of a night routine is to maximize your REM sleep to fully recharge your mind and body to then tackle your morning routine.

Here's an example of a night routine. I highly suggest starting with fewer things.

23:00:
"Evening Routine Alarm" ringtone.

23:00–23:40:
1) Hot shower and drink cold water after.
2) Brush my teeth.

23:40–00:00:
3) Journaling 5 minutes about a positive thing that happened that day.

NOT TO DO LIST:
Don't eat and check your phone after 20:30.
Don't plan & set goals of tomorrow after 18:00.
Don't eat heavy food or dairy for dinner.
Create your night routine.

The goal is to have at least 2 things for a night routine of 30 minutes.

From .... to .... (time):

NOT TO DO LIST:

9.3. IDEAL YEAR

The objective of an ideal year is to work between vacation, don't work for vacation. I recommend having a vacation for 10 days because 7 days is not enough, and 14 days is stagnating. Try to book yourself 5 vacations per year.

Here's an example of an ideal year.

JANUARY—FEBRUARY
- End of the 14 days holiday.
- 10 days off before the 2nd rush of the year.

MARCH—APRIL
- 2 months of hard execution.

MAY
- Mid-May 10 days spiritual retreat.

JUNE—JULY
- 2 months of planning/analyzing.
- 10-day nature trip at the end of July.

AUGUST—SEPTEMBER
- 2 months of hard execution.

OCTOBER
- 10-day discovery trip, mid October.

NOVEMBER—DECEMBER
- 1.5 months to finish the goals of the year.
- 14-day holiday family trip.

CREATE YOUR IDEAL YEAR.

From .... to .... (months):

....

....

From .... to .... (months):

....

....

From .... to .... (months):

....

....

From .... to .... (months):

....

....

From .... to .... (months):

....

....

9.4. IDEAL DAY

The objective of an ideal day is to satisfy the 7 wellness life dimensions.

Here's an example of an ideal day.

7:30—9:00:	Morning routine.
9:00—10:30:	Work at home on my one thing (Maker).
10:30—11:00:	Breakfast break.
11:00—12:30:	Work at home on my one thing (Maker).
12:30—13:00:	Walk, relax, read.
13:00—14:00:	Management, communication (Manager).
14:00—14:30:	Lunch break.
14:30—15:00:	Meditation and planning for the next day.
15:00—19:00:	Passion, learning, exploring.
19:00—20:30:	Dinner with friends.
20:30—23:00:	Relationship activities.
23:00—00:00:	Night routine.
00:00 – 7:30:	Sleep, 7 hours 30 minutes minimum.

CREATE YOUR IDEAL YEAR.

From .... to .... : ....

From .... to .... : ....

From .... to .... : ....

From .... to .... : ....

From .... to .... : ....

From .... to .... : ....

From .... to .... : ....

From .... to .... : ....

From .... to .... : ....

From .... to .... : ....

From .... to .... : ....

From .... to .... : ....

From .... to .... : ....

From .... to .... : ....

From .... to .... : ....

9.5. WEEKLY PLANNING TECHNIQUE

The objective of a week plan is to block periods of time per theme to not multi-task and also to open and close a cycle to evaluate our results.

PLANNING at the beginning of the week.
1. Set your intention for the week.
2. Set your 1 thing for the week.
3. Create your to-d list for the week.
4. Select the top 3 tasks for the week.
5. Set theme for the week and each day.

DELOADING at the beginning of the week.
1. What should I do?
2. What should someone else do?
3. Schedule it (block and tackle).

  Monday:
    Morning – Marketing
    Afternoon – Mentoring team (M)
    Night – New Projects
  Tuesday:
    Morning – Marketing
    Afternoon – Business Dev
    Night – New Projects
  Wednesday:
    Morning – Marketing
    Afternoon – Business Dev (M)
  Thursday:
    Morning – Admin & Structuring
    Afternoon – Business Dev
  Friday:
    Morning – Accounting & Finance
    Afternoon – Human Resource
  Sunday:
    Night – Coaching and Weekly Planning

REFLECTING at the end of the week.
1. What is the progress on my one thing?
2. Where did I feel uncomfortable?
3. Knowing what I know now, what would I do differently?
4. Where did I win last week?

Dreamer Mode
3 YEARS OF PERSONAL LIFE VISION

10.1. WRITTEN VERSION IN THE PRESENT TENSE

🕐 30 minutes to complete

A 3-year vision written in the present tense mentioning your personality, criteria of your relationships, purpose, your why, habits, values, virtues, fears, experiences, location, situation, work, business, finance, spirituality, physical, community, etc.

In 20........ (year), I am in .... (location, type of environment)

with ....

.... (family, friends, lover, type of person)

....

....

....

....

....

....

....

....

....

10.2. MAKE A VISION BOARD AND DREAM BOOK

🕐 30 minutes to complete

https://medium.com/@jfbrou/create-this-pocket-dream-book-to-become-your-best-version-fef9c6c1305

This is why cavemen drew their dinners on the rocks before hunting. Use canva.com to translate your vision visually with photos, quotes, statements, models, drawing, colors, etc. Carry this visualization tool with you every day or hang it where you'll see it daily. For the moment, put 2 photos for each of the ideal 7 life dimensions vision.

10.3. 3-YEAR VISION OF HELL

🕐 30 minutes to complete

Write an opposite 3-year vision of HELL of how your life will be if you don't act on solving your problems, realizing your dreams, facing your fears, and living with purpose.

Peace Mode
GRATITUDE & AFFIRMATION STATEMENT

11.1. GRATITUDE ENUMERATION

🕐 10 minutes to complete

We need a vision to grow, but we need to be grounded, grateful, and humble of what we have been through, and of what we have now. Our goal is to live in the now at every situation, moment, second while blocking time for planning, visualizing, and asking the universe. Act like you'll die tomorrow, grow like you'll live for 100 years. Write a 5-10-line gratitude statement of your life right now.

....

....

....

....

....

....

....

....

....

....

....

....

11.2. I AM AFFIRMATIONS STATEMENT

🕐 5 minutes to complete

Strengthen yourself with I AM affirmations every day. (Physical, Mental, Emotional)

I AM ....

I AM ....

I AM ....

I AM ....

I AM ....

I AM ....

I AM ....

I AM ....

I AM ....

11.3. SELF-LOVE LETTER

....

....

....

....

....

....

Conclusion

Wow, you have done it !!!

Now it's time to jump and fail as much as possible toward your vision. It's the only way, consistency every day, never ever give up, be hopeful, keep the excitement flowing and always be grateful for the journey.

Here's my best advice to jump and fail often. The best way to build your 7 wellness life dimensions is to build a community around your personality, purpose, values, vision, and passions. Serve yourself as a client of your company, you'll know the market by heart.

This could easily become a business if you push hard and never give up or it can be turned into a non-profit or it can stay small to satisfy your personal life.

Thank you so much for doing this workbook, it means everything to me. I've put all my love and experiences here to hopefully make an impact. I hope you can share it with your friends and family so you can all push each other to greater heights. Please don't forget to write an Amazon review, your support means everything.

Jf Brou

Xoxo

If you need anything, don't hesitate. I'm here for you.

But remember, all the answers are inside you. Meditate.

Personal Notes:

Appendix 1

100 PRODUCTIVITY TRICKS THEY WILL NEVER TEACH YOU IN THE UNIVERSITY

PERSONAL

1. Self-Development Journal: Journal every day analyzing your thought process, introspecting your behaviors and emotions, doing exercises, taking notes on what you've learned, listing gratitudes and affirmations. Book: 4 hours work week / Tim Ferriss

2. Stack Dominos: Goal set someday, then 10 years, 5 years, and 3 years and bring it back to year goal, quarter goal, month goal, week goal, and day goal.

3. Morning Routine: Prime your brain toward getting into a momentum, put happy vibe music on, drink cold water, do a 2-minute workout yoga or stretching to activate your brain's reactive system, do a 5-minute journal affirmation, do positive statements of love and gratitude, 20 minutes bodyweight, take a cold shower, drink some cold-pressed green juice and eat fruits.

4. The 1st 10 Minutes of Your Day: This is a crucial moment when your brain is functioning with the highest amount of brain waves. Everything you hear, think, or see will imprint onto your spirit for the rest of your day. Tune in to the right state of mind in the first 10 minutes of your day with mental positive affirmation and a gratitude statement.

5. Sleep: You need 7 to 8 hours a night to get 5 hours of REM Sleep. Try some earplugs, eye cover, and a warm and fluffy blanket. Book: The sleep revolution / Arianna Huffington

6. Control Your Sleep Thieves: Don't drink coffee before 12:00, don't eat dinner after 8:30, don't use your mind as a memory device, don't watch porn or drama movie/series, don't look at a screen 30 minutes before sleep, etc.

7. Night Routine: The goal is to empty your mind and relax your body. Don't eat and check your phone after 21:00, don't plan and set goals for tomorrow after 19:00, and don't eat heavy food for dinner on weekdays, or take a hot shower and drink cold water after, and try journaling 5 minutes about a positive thing that happened that day, do 10 minutes of sleep meditation lying in bed while doing muscle contractions.

8. Bed Time: Go to bed between 8-10 pm, around 2 hours after the sun goes down. Our body is connected with the energy of the sun.

9. Life-Changing Habits: Build one life-changing habit at a time for 66 days using the Kaizen principle. We can only build 5 life-changing habits a year. If you chase 2 rabbits at a time you'll catch either of them.

10. Trigger Behaviors: Set alarms with triggers to act on habits or things you want to improve and then link it to a reward to build the habit loop.

11. Photo Accountability: Use Google Photo to track your daily habits, workout, diet, social life, etc.

12. Settle in 1 location: stay 60-90 days in 1 destination with your steady Airbnb and coworking place in the neighborhood. 20+ minutes of commuting to work can lead to depression.
13. Dopamine: Maximize your energy by consuming less dopamine like notifications, drugs, sex, etc.
14. NOFAP: No porn, no Tinder, no Instagram. It creates problems with your neurotransmitter because too much dopamine is being released.
15. Announce Your Goal Publicly: Write on social media, make a video of what you'll do too. Send it to your friends and post it on all social media sites you subscribe to.
16. Unconscious Addictions: Remove them 1 by 1. Things that you do too much without realizing it steal your time for the other 7 wellness life dimensions. Ex: burying yourself too much in books.
17. Affirmation/Self-Talk: We have a constant conversation running all the time (The Monkey Mind). We have 50k-70k thoughts a day, of which 80% are negative. You need to control all micro negative self-talk and turn them into positive ones.
18. Learn 60 Minutes Every Day: 30 minutes in the morning and 30 minutes at night or while commuting. Find your golden nugget of the day and write it down in your journal.
19. Don't Commute More than 20 Minutes: Studies show that people who commute or drive more than 20 minutes to get to work are more depressed.
20. Consistency: 5 minutes a day is better than 30 minutes 3 times a week. This is according to the Kaizen principle.
21. How are you Living: You won an ultra-lottery of being alive, 1 chance out of 400 trillion compare to winning the lottery is 1 out of 14 million and getting struck by lightning is 1 out of 10 million, and being killed in a plane crash is 1 out of 11 million.
22. Visualization: Create a pocket dream book or board in your room with images, goals, quotes, models of inspiration, and the things you want.
23. Your Face Muscles: Tense forehead muscles with crusty eyes will lead to more stress and less peace. Make sure you are always smiling from the inside with your lips slightly inclined up to attract positive people.
24. Your Environment: Your flatmate or house companion might be affecting your vibrations. The city or island you live in, and the weather and how comfortable you are also affects your state of mind.

JOB

25. Willpower: It's like a phone battery, start the day at 100%. Be aware, manage it and recharge it smartly. These things drain your willpower: Implementing new behavior, filtering distractions, resisting temptation, suppressing emotions, restraining aggression, suppressing impulses, taking tests, trying to impress others, coping with fear, doing something you don't like to do, selecting long-term over short-term results, etc. Book: The willpower Instinct / Kelly McGonigal
26. Your ONE THING: Every morning for 3-4 hours, work on your one thing that will lead you to extraordinary results. Everything else is a distraction and drains your willpower. Be a maker in the morning and a manager in the afternoon. Book: The One Thing / Gary Kelly
27. Work from Home: Work from home the first 3 hours of the day to EAT THAT FROG. Book: Eat That Frog / Brian Tracy
28. Physical Workplace: Empty and clean your desk and have a strong back cover. Work with a wall in front of you so you won't be distracted by people passing by. Every 3 minutes workers get distracted and it takes 11 minutes to get back in focus. Book: Getting things done / David Allen

29. Wi-Fi & Desk: Chase 20mbps or more Wi-Fi, carry a pocket Wi-Fi, get an unlimited sim card. Work from a steady desk with a chair with a good back cover.

30. The 80/20 Pareto Law: The Pareto law states that roughly 80% of the effects come from 20% of the causes. Analyze every detail of your life and work with it to focus on what matters.

31. Pomodoro Technique: Do a minimum of 8 blocks of 25 minutes per day. Your brain can only work with a focus of 90 minutes at the time with a peak of concentration at 45 minutes.

32. Multitasking: Never ever multitask, it's the most toxic thing for your productivity. You lose 20% of your time in a day. Having 2 windows open on your computer at the same time is a form of multitasking

33. Track Everything: Track your work with Toggl/Desktime/Hubstaff and do your finances weekly with Mint and go over your goals with an accountability partner.

34. Flow/Deep Work: Your ideal massive goal is to train yourself to go into flow/deep work every day. Book: Deep Work: Rules for Focused Success in a Distracted World / Cal Newport; FLOW: The Psychology of optimal experience / Mihaly Csikszentmihalyi

35. 432hz Music: Listen to it while working or going to sleep (classic, guitar, instrumental, movie trailer). If you are working and listening to music with lyrics, you are multitasking because your subconscious tries to process those words even if you don't understand the language.

36. Emails are toxic: Master the email game to do email 3h/week. Filtering, labelling, using 2 addresses, using an autoresponder. Don't show the email Google Chrome extension and block site extensions in the morning and at night.

37. Accountability Partner: Find an accountability partner or coach, log in daily and track your evolution. HabitBull mobile app.

38. Motivation is Garbage: Trick your brain to act within the 5-second rule. Tedtalk: How to stop screwing yourself over | Mel Robbins

39. Be Agile: Constantly analyze your time at hand with your resources and willpower level to see if a 5-minute specific task could be done.

40. Success Brings More Success: Reach the momentum principle of success.

41. Finish it Now: Finish the task at hand now so you don't lose 500% of your time.

42. Tomorrow Goal Planning: Plan tomorrow today before quitting work. It's only 10 minutes of your work session.

43. Give up Perfection: Launch publicly at 80% done, put your ego aside and ask for feedback from your targeted audience.

44. No Watch Day: Battle manic-depression with worry breaks with no watch.

45. Worries are an Illusion: Worries = stress = burnout = depression = hard to do anything productive.

46. Your #1 Professional Skill: Master and improve it constantly. This is what you are paid for, this is how you bring the greatest value to your organization. The average CEO works 28 minutes a day on it. The Compound Effect / Darren Hardy

47. You're Being Paid to Rest: Maximize sleep and off times, playtime, hobbies, social life, and stabilize your 7 wellness life dimensions. Don't work to go on vacation, live in vacation and take breaks going to work. Plan your vacation calendar for the next 12 months with 2 months of work sessions in-between.

48. Improve 1 Skill at a Time: There's too much knowledge and information out there. Every 4 months focus on 1 skill by learning and acting on the top books, Ted talks, podcasts, and YouTube tutorials.

49. Emergency Channel: Set up one that only a vital few know about. Use different chat apps with notifications that you use with those rare people.

BUSINESS

50. Start with Why: List 20 reasons why you will never give up. Book/Ted Talk: Start With Why / Simon Sinek

51. Leaders Eat Last: Let other people express their opinions first, it will help their sense of involvement without affecting their perspective and allow you to have the perspective of everyone before you express your opinion. Book/Ted Talk: Leaders eat last / Simon Sinek

52. Voice vs Typing: Send voice messages (220 words/minute) instead of writing (70 words/minute). 80% of the web will be audio and video by 2020, now 30% of Google searches are made by voice.

53. Record Screencast: Make a mini video training recording your screen while talking to show exactly one thing to get done right instead of planning a meeting for it. Use the Loom extension.

54. Hire Slowly and Fire Quickly: You are better off finding someone fitting your values and your company's culture than one having the best CV. Enthusiasm and commitment are better than skills. A badly managed employee will end up costing you 4 times his salary over a period of 12 months.

55. Written/Text Message: Never ever bring up concerns via text message. Message only to give respect to humans.

56. Set Up All Expectations: Set up expectations for all coworkers, clients, and suppliers with clear announcement automation.

PHYSICAL

57. Drink Water: Get water and prepare to not have to break your flow, at least 2 liters per day of filtered water. Don't trust the corporation selling you bad water. Carry your water in a blue bottle with crystal at the bottom.

58. Exercise: 20 minutes minimum daily to re-oxygenate your mind.

59. What the Health: Eat on your own self-aware terms. Food is your carburetor. If after eating you don't feel more energized, you didn't eat real food, or you ate too much. Eat for 20 minutes and until you feel you are 80% full.

60. Stress/Fears/Doubt Free: Stress is the biggest killer of dreams. When you are stressed you can't think, you can't work, and you can't have energy.

61. Fasting: Water fasting for 3 days for 2-3 times a year can give you 20 years of longevity. Read in-depth about it, and make sure to break your fast properly.

62. Coffee Enema: All disease come from the gut. Clean your colon with the German technique recommended by the cancer research institute.

63. Don't Eat Badly Treated Animals: When you eat dead animals that were badly beaten up and raised with no care, you eat their attitude, stress, and suffering. Stop eating any kind of meat for 10 days then eat it for only a day and you'll see the devastating realization on your thought patterns.

64. Regulate Legal Drugs: Salt, Refined Sugar, Caffeine, Alcohol, Nicotine. All these should be consumed as little as possible to keep a balanced mind.

FINANCE

65. 5% Love Account: Collect a little bit weekly and always give it in-person quarterly to an initiative that you really care about. And you need to see in person the people benefiting from it. Book: Give and Take / Adam Grant

66. Pay Yourself First: Pay yourself 10% of your monthly income before all other monthly bills. Put the 10% pay in an investment account. Book: The Richest Man in Babylon / George Clason

67. Outsourcing: Outsource all your handy tasks in the Philippines, India, Eastern Europe, Colombia, and Venezuela. Search on Upwork.com or Onlinejobs.ph or Indeed specifically in those countries.

68. Personal Assistant: Use one to buy, search, book, schedule, remind, and contact. You can find an assistant on Upwork.

69. Weekly Finance Report: Take 30 minutes to analyze and give feedback each Sunday. MINT App

70. Invest Your Savings: Every quarter or semester invest your $5,000 and pay yourself first by putting your savings into a project linked to your resources.

RELATIONSHIP

71. Find Mentors: Seek advice from people who have achieved 10% more than you have.

72. Masterminds: Gather 2-3 friends into a weekly 1-hour mastermind to build on things you have learned and support each other.

73. Build Your Community: Building your community is the most fulfilling way to satisfy your social life and the best way to start a business.

74. Become a Massive LOVER: Hug everyone you care about with your head on the right side to have a heart to heart connection.

75. Say No Gracefully: When you know where you are going, it is easy to see what can help you get to your destination or not. From that point you'll hardly have to say no to very many opportunities.

76. Everyone is Insecure: At every level people don't know what they are doing. Everyone is trying to figure it out. So, don't care about what other people think.

77. Praising Someone: Send out 3-4 minutes personal video messages praising someone for their support or work and it will give you a massive energy boost.

78. Your Top 5: The person you'll be in 5 years is based on the 5 people you hang out with the most and the books you read today. Make a life audit to spend more time with your top 5.

SPIRITUAL

79. Minimalist Lifestyle: Stop worrying for stuff to free up your mental bandwidth.

80. Meditate Daily: Meditate daily to control your mind's wandering and negative thoughts.

81. 7 Wellness Life Dimensions: Satisfy your 7 dimensions one at a time choosing the one that can affect the other at the same time. These are Finance, Spiritual, Personal, Job, Business, Relationship, and Physical.

82. Power of Now: It's the only thing that is real. Books: The Power of Now / Eckhart Tolle; The Compass of Now / DDnard, Be here now / Ram Dass

83. Be a Teacher: Teaching is the end of the circle of learning. There's always someone in your entourage to inspire, mentor, and support mentally.

84. Find Your Temple: The gym, meditation room, library/bookstore. We all need these places to go evacuate our worries and doubts when things get dark.

85. 100% Responsible: We are the problem and the solution all at the same time.

86. Creative Procrastination: There's always one thing we love that we do too much.

87. We are all Procrastinators: Know when to stop it and break the cycle. Set a daily due date. Tedtalk: Inside the mind of a master procrastinator | Tim Urban

88. True Wealth: Don't chase recognition, trophies, money, or fame. Real success is about how many people you serve, it's about how many lives you positively affect. Start small with your sister/brother and parents. It will make you fly.

89. Don't be a Copycat: Take a bit of what you like from everybody.

90. Listen Mindfully: Humans can talk on average 220 words a minute but can process 550 words a minute, that's why your mind wanders when you listen to someone or listen with the intent of responding. Listening mindfully creates deep human connections.

91. Control Your Decisions: Disable all notifications and put Adblock on your laptop and Browser AdBlock on your phone, download music on your phone instead of YouTube or Spotify with ads. The goal is to find ways that you hear about them 8 times. Show your phone who is the boss of your life.

92. Write Everything Down on Paper: Cognitive reaction frees up your mind. You want to do everything you can to not use your mind as a memory device.

93. Self-Talk: Control your self-talk so as to be constantly optimistic and positive. Micro negative self-talk is a soul killer.

94. Change Your Words, Change Your Life: Stop saying "I don't have time," or "I am too busy." Make the time. We always have time to do what we like. Stop saying "I can't afford that" and make a plan to afford it.

95. Your Major Key Constraints: Empty your bag of rocks. What is holding you back? What past wounds are you still carrying in your day to day life?

96. Weapons of Mass Distraction: Remove the temptation and track your behavior using Block App, Rescue Time, News Feed Eradicator, and Plane Mode.

97. Clean up Virtual Space: Clean up your Google Drive, Favoris, hard drive, and social accounts to free up your mind and feel lighter.

98. Deconstruct Your Ego: Ego is your enemy / Ryan Holiday. If your ego is too big it will lead you to a dangerous path that will always backfire on you. Live an immersive spiritual experience of more than 10 days to start the deconstruction.

99. Access the Spiritual Dimension: An Ayahuasca retreat or smoking DMT will lead you to comprehend your deepest demons, your most oppressive thoughts, the spiritual dimension and even experience death.

100. The Dharma lifestyle: Make a 10-day vipassana silent meditation retreat to learn this unique 2,500-year-old technique to access the universe inside you.

Appendix 2

TIPS

Top books to read to start your journey toward mastery:
1 - Think and Grow Rich by Napoleon Hill
2 - The 4-hour workweek by Tim Ferriss
3 - The One Thing by Gary Keller
4 - The Power of Now by Eckhart Tolle
5 - How to win friends and influence people by Dale Carnegie
6 - Rich Dad Poor Dad by Robert T. Kiyosaki
7 - Start with Why by Simon Sinek

Top Productivity Chrome Extensions:
1 - Facebook News Feed Eradicator (Access your email without seeing the Facebook news feed.)
2 - Inbox When Ready for Gmail (Access your email without seeing if you have new inbox.)
3 - Block Site (Block weapons of mass distraction at a specific time and day.)
4 - Toggl (Time tracker for work with Pomodoro.)
5 - Adblock Plus (Block ads everywhere on the web.)
7 - LastPass (No need to remember your passwords anymore.)
8 - Rescue Time (Analyze the amount of time you pass on the web and per site.)
9 - Evernote web clipper (Save everything quickly.)

Top Productivity Mobile Apps:
1 - Block Apps (Block weapons of mass distraction at a specific time and day)
2 - Rescue Time (Analyze the amount of time you pass on your phone and per app.)
3 - LastPass (No need to remember passwords anymore.)
4 - Habit Tracker (Track your habits one at a time.)
4 - Voice Recorder (Empty your mind with voice notes and long voice messages/emails.)
5 - Fabulous (Motivation app to change behavior - I don't use it anymore but try it.)

Top Productivity Business Tools:
1 - Monday.com (Project Management and Communication) (Check also Airtable, Trello)
2 - Loom (Record quick screencast video for better team communication.)
3 - Slack (Communication with bots and reminder - we don't use it anymore, only monday.com.)
4 - Hubstaff (Team tracker per member and project - we just moved to Toggl.)
5 - Zoom (Video conference call that you can record - new feature reporting interview statistics.)
6 - Google Drive (Collaborate on building documents.)
7 - Xero or Quickbooks (Get in-depth reports of your finance on your phone.)

Appendix 3

3 THINGS SUCCESSFUL PEOPLE HAVE IN COMMON

Practice meditation daily
(Objective: Control the monkey mind & emotion awareness)

We have 50k-70k thoughts a day, 80% of which are negative.
2 minutes a day for beginners
3 days water Fasting
10 days Vipassana or Transcendental Meditation
Ayahuasca

Write in a self-development journal daily
(Objective: Read the pages of your own book to control the patterns.)

3 Gratitude statements
Affirmation/Self-Talk
Podcast/Books notes
Introspection exercises
Dream remembering
Excited for tomorrow
Positive stories/events

Have a life coach or a mentor
(Objective: Advice, accountability and tracking your evolution.)

APPS: coach.me; Remente; Primed Mind
Books: Blinkist; MentorBox
Search: table.co; clarity.fm; upwork, LinkedIn
Certified Coach (Tony Robbins, John Maxwell, Brian Tracy)

Become Workbook Serie 1
Second Edition

For information about permission to reproduce selections,
contact: info@interstude.com.

Interior Design: Staci Weber
Front & Back Cover: https://www.fiverr.com/kozakura
Proofreader & Editor: https://www.fiverr.com/iluv2proofread

ISBN-13: 978-1-7347082-0-2

www.jfbrou.com